Witches

Witches
by Rhoda Blumberg

Franklin Watts
New York / London / Toronto / 1979
A First Book

Cover photograph by: Carole Bertol
Cover design by: Ginger Giles

Photographs courtesy of: New York Public Library Picture Collection: title page, pp. 3, 4, 7, 8 (left and right), 13, 14, 20, 23, 28, 31, 36, 39, 40; Metropolitan Museum of Art: p. 17; United Press International: pp. 45, 46; National Collection of Fine Arts, Smithsonian Institution: p. 51.

Library of Congress Cataloging in Publication Data

Blumberg, Rhoda.
Witches.

(A First book)
Bibliography: p.
Includes index.
SUMMARY: Describes witches and witchcraft in history and in fiction from ancient times up to the modern resurgence of the "witch business."
1. Witchcraft—Juvenile literature. [1. Witchcraft] I. Title.
BF1566.B57   133.4   79-1427
ISBN 0-531-02948-4

Copyright © 1979 by Rhoda Blumberg
All rights reserved
Printed in the United States of America
6 5 4 3 2 1

Contents

THE WORLD OF WITCHES 1

Ancient Witches 5

THE WAR AGAINST WITCHES 11

Finding Witches 15
The Pact with the Devil 15
The Sabbat 16

Examining Witches 19

Sentencing Witches 21

The Death Toll 22

BRITISH WITCHES 25

English Witches 26
The Water Test 27
Imps and Witch Marks 27

Scottish Witches 30

WITCHES IN AMERICA 33

Salem, the Devil's Headquarters 35
The Witch List 37
Spooky Proof 41
The Touch Test 41

WITCHES TODAY 43

The Witch Religion 44
The Modern Coven 47

Evil Witches 49

Tribal Witches 50

The Witch Business 52

GLOSSARY 55

BIBLIOGRAPHY 57

INDEX 60

FOR MY COVEN:

Betty, Gladys, Murray, Mickey,
Herbert, Mimi, Sydney, Estelle,
Bernard, Norma, Lee,
and Jerry-the-Warlock

Witches

The World of Witches

Most of us think of witches as fairy tale characters, usually ugly old women bent with age and intent upon doing evil. Sometimes we picture them as Halloween hags riding broomsticks by the light of the moon. But witches are not fly-by-night storybook characters. They are real people who are supposed to be able to harm or help others through their own magical, supernatural powers.

Witches exist all over the world today. They perform their craft not only in the jungles of Asia and Africa but in the cities of Europe and America. They sing chants and mutter spells that are supposed to work magic for good or evil. Fortune-telling, advising the troubled, mixing love potions, and making medicines are a few of their many activities. Although some are known as good witches who try to help people, most witches are feared as evil-doers who bewitch others.

Those who call themselves witches have always performed their skills as a business or hobby. However, they have been outnumbered by those called witches by others. Thousands of innocent people were killed because they were accused of evil magic. These so-called witches were dreamed up by political and religious enemies and by superstitious and spiteful people.

People were falsely accused of witchcraft. They were charged with using curses and spells to raise storms, sink ships, spoil crops, create accidents, and cause disease. They were condemned for possessing an *evil eye*, which enabled them to harm with a stare or kill with a glare.

In addition to causing major disasters, they supposedly amused themselves by doing minor mischief, such as souring milk, putting fleas in peas, causing nightmares, and creating lovers' quar-

Witches and witchcraft have never been limited to only the Western World, as you can see from this Japanese print of an Oriental witch.

Male witches, sometimes called wizards or warlocks, were often no more popular than their female counterparts. This engraving done in 1872 is entitled "Adam Warner Hooted As A Wizard."

rels. Their recipes for cooking up evil included bats' blood, babies' bodies, and dead people's flesh. It was believed by many that witches enjoyed harming people because they delighted in the misery of others.

Blaming witches for bad luck was an easy way of explaining everything from business failures to floods and fires. If witches could be stopped from doing evil, all would be right with the world.

Although mostly women were accused of being witches, boys and girls were also denounced, and in some places male witches were more common than female witches. Male witches are sometimes called *warlocks* or *wizards*.

Most frightening was that anyone could be called a witch. According to popular belief, witches spent most of their lives looking and acting like ordinary people. A friend, the person next door, even a close relative could be living a double life: a plain Joe or Josephine by day, and a super-human horror by night.

How could anyone know who was a witch? Witches were said to *shape-shift*: they could appear as beautiful women or as pitiful beggars. They could even transform themselves into beasts and insects. No one ever watched these quick-change artists, because their hocus-pocus was performed in secret, and they became invisible whenever they wished.

Those who called themselves witches and those called witches by others have been part of history since ancient times.

ANCIENT WITCHES

Thousands of years ago male and female witches in Babylonia, Egypt, and Assyria claimed magical powers that enabled them to forecast the future. They scanned the stars, studied the flights of birds, examined the entrails of animals, the palms, freckles, and footprints of people, and used countless other ways to forecast coming events. Witches also sold curses, blessings, medicines, love potions, and poisons. Kings and commoners paid for their services.

The ancient Hebrews also believed in witches. The Bible's commandment "Thou shalt not suffer a witch to live" became the excuse for horrible witch hunts in Europe and America. During Biblical times, it probably caused the death of many who dabbled in magic.

Greek witches bowed down to Hecate, the ugly goddess of the moon and the dead. People claimed that followers of Hecate could change themselves into foxes or flies; that they summoned ghosts, made poisons, and drove people mad; that they were so dreadful they ate dead bodies. Thessaly was the region in Greece noted for its many witches.

There were also good Greek witches whose spells and chants blessed everything from crops to foreign wars. Some specialized in selling *windbags* to sailors. Breezes able to speed voyages of the biggest ships were contained in cloth sacks that were closed by a series of knots. Whenever a knot was untied, a gust of wind escaped. Witches' windbags were prized possessions. When one failed to work, sailors supposed either that the bag had been cursed or that a phony witch had fooled them into making a bad buy.

Many Romans feared both good and bad witchcraft. Several emperors banned witches from the land—except for those witches who could be useful to them. From time to time suspected male and female witches were hurled from cliffs to their deaths.

Witches were thought to have great influence over the weather. Here, a wizard attempts to sell sailors the wind tied up in three knots of rope.

Left: a wizard condemned to death during the Inquisition. Before he was killed, he was forced to wear a shirt and hat on which were painted devils, flames, and human heads.

Below: an Italian woodcut from the 17th century depicts followers of witchcraft stepping over a cross. Note their eyes are closed, signifying that they have shut their eyes to God.

Europe's first big witch hunt took place in Rome during the fourth century A.D., when Emperor Valens doomed anyone attempting magic. Even those who used herbs to heal the sick were executed. A boy who tried "magic words" to stop his own stomachache was sentenced to death.

Witches like those of Greece and Rome lived in the forests and fields of France, Germany, and Britain. Christian missionaries who made journeys throughout Europe found them everywhere.

Harmful magic was, of course, unchristian. But folk witches who acted as doctors were also condemned, because Christians believed that true help could come only to those who sought the church's aid.

Missionaries called pagan gods demons—evil spirits ruled by the Devil. The word *witch* acquired a new meaning. It meant anyone who received supernatural powers directly from the Devil or, indirectly, from pagan gods.

During the first twelve centuries of Christianity people accused of witchcraft rarely received harsh punishments. They were told to repent or to fast because they had sinned. Sometimes they paid a fine or served a short prison term. However, since local leaders had the power to punish, witches were at times sentenced to death.

Widespread witch hunts started after the Inquisition was set up by the Roman Catholic church during the thirteenth century. *Inquisition* means *inquiry* or *investigation*. Its purpose was finding and punishing heretics. *Heretics* were those who didn't believe in all the teachings of the church. Because witches were called the Devil's servants they were enemies of God, and therefore they were classed as heretics. The Inquisition tortured and burned them.

During the fourteenth century a plague known as the Black Death killed one-third of the people of Europe. Witches were accused of poisoning wells and, in league with the Devil, of spreading the plague.

During the fourteenth and fifteenth centuries the number of demons and witches multiplied. Europe seemed to be overrun by them. Mass executions were common at the time that Columbus discovered America. Witch burnings and hangings continued to kill thousands of innocent people for hundreds of years.

The War Against Witches

The Hammer of Witches, published in 1486, plotted war against witches by instructing readers how to find, convict, and kill them. Written by two monks, Henry Kramer and Jackob Sprenger, it was an easy-to-read, handy, "how-to-do-it" guide. The book was an instant success. It became so popular that many editions appeared in German, Italian, and English. From its first appearance until the middle of the eighteenth century, it was used as an official handbook by Catholic and Protestant judges.

The Hammer of Witches was an insanely cruel book. The authors seemed to delight in describing methods of torture and in advising their readers that anybody suspected of witchcraft deserved to be burned at the stake. They even recommended using green wood to make the fires burn slower, because witches deserved to die in prolonged agony.

Inspired by *The Hammer of Witches,* judges wrote books adding brutal details about fighting the witch war. In his *Demonology,* published in 1595, Judge Nicholas Remy of France advised others to follow his example. He sentenced the children of condemned witches to be "stripped and beaten with rods round the place where their parents were being burned alive."

Judge Benedict Carpzov of Germany suggested seventeen different methods of torture, including driving wooden wedges under the fingernails and then setting fire to the wedges. Because he had presided over thousands of trials, he was considered an authority. As late as 1728 his book was quoted in court, when a judge sentenced a so-called witch to death.

Anyone who questioned court decisions or witch manuals was in danger of being burned at the stake. Even judges who seemed too easy on their prisoners were killed. Such was the fate

Various manners of torturing heretics during the Inquisition.

This 17th-century French engraving shows a meeting at which the devil was worshipped in the form of a goat.

of Judge Dietrich Flade, who was also the head of a German university. Because he released a suspected witch, the prince of his district had him arrested, tortured, strangled, and burned.

FINDING WITCHES

Men, women, and children were warned to look out for any telltale signs of witches at work. Duke Maximilian of Bavaria was one of the many rulers who declared it a crime *not to report* anyone suspected of witchcraft. And the accusers didn't have to worry about being hated; their names were kept secret. They never had to face the person they accused, nor did they have to undergo cross-examination. Their statements were never challenged. Suspected witches usually were not allowed to have lawyers or witnesses to defend them. In districts where lawyers for witches were allowed, none dared to appear, because defending a witch made the person a "witch lover." That was as bad as being a witch.

Many mentally ill people were thought to be witches or bewitched. Most doctors believed that only Satan could cause insanity. Even people who were so upset that they talked to themselves were accused of carrying on conversations with evil spirits.

There were also mentally ill men and women who really believed they were witches. One woman confessed that she had murdered a baby and had given the baby's body to the Devil. Although the baby was found safe with its mother, the woman was hanged because she lied and because she thought like a witch!

The Pact with the Devil
Catholics and Protestants believed that all witches made a contract, or *pact*, with the Devil. Witches agreed to worship and

serve the Devil in return for supernatural powers. The pact, written with witches' blood, could be made during a secret meeting with the Devil, who could appear suddenly, anywhere, and in a variety of shapes. According to one thirteen-year-old girl, Satan leaped out of a jar, grew like a genie, and tried to sign her up as his servant.

Most pacts were signed at *sabbats*, imaginary events that were said to take place four times a year, once each season. Men, women, and children were condemned to death merely because they were suspected of having been to a sabbat.

The Sabbat

A sabbat was an assembly of witches headed by the Devil. Witches were supposed to have sneaked from their homes to attend these gatherings, slipping through keyholes or door cracks, or sweeping up chimneys on brooms. They were also thought to fly through the night sky on pitchforks, shovels, goats, cats, dragons, airships, and assorted strange-looking UFOs. Newcomers to Satan's secret society became members by signing pacts with their blood—a red-letter night. In return for a promise to serve the Devil, they received magical powers enabling them to harm others.

After new members were welcomed, everybody feasted, danced, and made merry in all sorts of shameful ways. Human-sized toads were sometimes dance partners, and babies boiled in

"The Witches' Sabbat," a woodcut by Hans Baldung from the 16th century.

bubbling cauldrons made a popular banquet dish. Sabbats ended when the cocks crowed at daybreak. Then it was "fly-away-home" time.

Sabbats were big conventions. Witnesses claimed to have seen one hundred thousand people on a mountaintop at an international congress of witches in the French Alps.

Witches were also believed to attend meetings called *covens*. Covens were small local get-togethers usually made up of twelve witches plus the Devil or a demon.

Because it was thought that children sometimes accompanied their witch parents to covens and sabbats, they were sought as witnesses. In many cases they were forced to testify against their mothers and fathers. One judge recommended burning boys and girls with hot irons to make them talk. Some children dreamed up stories about covens and sabbats. The most shocking part was that adults believed these tall stories.

One of the most horrifying events in witchcraft history took place in the town of Mora, Sweden, in 1669. Three hundred children supposedly attended a witches' sabbat. When the king of Sweden heard about it he appointed a royal commission to investigate. Children talked about flying to the Devil on monkeys, goats, horses, and sleeping men.

Twelve days after the royal commission arrived in Mora, twenty-three women were burned together in one fire—an event that was celebrated by the town's population. The next day Mora had another big fire when fifteen boys were roasted to death. Forty-seven so-called witches were sent to a nearby village where they were burned. In addition, fifty-six young boys and girls were sentenced to a variety of punishments, such as prison or whippings in public every Sunday for a year.

EXAMINING WITCHES

After being arrested, witches were stripped of their clothing and their heads and bodies were shaved. The judge and his assistants looked for charms that might be concealed in clothing and demons that hid in hair. The main purpose of the head-to-toe search was to locate the *Devil's mark*. All witches were supposed to have been marked after they signed the pact with the Devil. Freckles, scars, and pimples were pointed to as Devil's marks.

Suspected witches were questioned and tortured as quickly as possible. Speed was necessary so that Satan wouldn't have time to coach the prisoner and prevent a confession. The whip, the rack, thumbscrews and other bone crushers, red-hot pincers, boiling water baths, and other terrible tortures were used to extract "the truth." Witch houses with torture chambers were built in many towns. In a special witch house in Bamberg, Germany, over six hundred witches were tortured and burned.

Victims were not asked *what* crimes they had committed, but rather *why* they had committed certain crimes. Lists of questions developed myths about witches' evil deeds and about goings-on at sabbats. Typical questions required short answers or were phrased for "yes-or-no" replies. For example, "How long have you been a witch?" "Can you change yourself into a wolf?" "Can you raise storms?" "How many children have you murdered?"

Victims were tortured until they admitted their guilt. After confession, if they changed their minds and declared their innocence, they were tortured again. One woman was tortured fifty-six times, until she died.

After confessing, prisoners were forced to supply names of other witches. Records show that one woman, racked with pain from constant torture, accused 150 others of witchcraft.

Two 15th-century witches burn a chicken and a snake, causing a shower of rain.

That handy handbook, *The Hammer of Witches,* instructed judges to promise mercy if a prisoner confessed and supplied the names of other witches. After receiving a full confession, the judge was to keep his word. The book instructed him to show mercy by leaving the courtroom and allowing another judge to pronounce the death sentence.

SENTENCING WITCHES

Witches were frequently carried about in baskets, so that their feet would not touch the ground and shoot evil rays into the earth. They were sometimes led into court backward to prevent their evil eyes from glaring at the judge and bewitching him. Prisoners who confessed, either voluntarily or under torture, received the mercy of being strangled before they were burned. Those who insisted they were innocent were burned alive.

An execution was a public spectacle. In many towns trumpets blared and church bells rang as everyone rushed to the main square to watch the "fireworks." Children were excused from school to witness witch burnings. School choirs sang hymns as bodies were pulled by chains into the flames and burned to ashes.

In France and Germany and Scotland the prisoner or the prisoner's family paid the cost of imprisonment, trial, and execution. Complete expense accounts list the cost of meals in prison, fees paid to torturers, the price of torture instruments, wood for the stake, and the salaries of the executioner and court officials.

Three women who were burned alive in 1595 received in advance the following bill for three days' expenses, from their sentencing to the day of their execution:

33 florins	for feeding and housing the prisoners and their guards
14 florins	for the executioner
32 florins	for entertainment and a banquet for the judges and their staff (which took place *after* the trial).

Even after a burning, officials had a banquet that was paid for with the victim's money.

Innkeepers, judges, and executioners made money. Town officials who made a practice of grabbing all the property that belonged to condemned witches became rich. Witch killings were good for business.

THE DEATH TOLL

Europe's insane witch hunt raged, especially during the sixteenth and seventeenth centuries. One hundred and thirty-three witches burned together in Saxony. People visiting France reported seeing thousands of stakes to which witches were bound. For several years the city of Cologne in Germany averaged three hundred burnings a year. Whole villages in Switzerland and Germany were erased from the map after their citizens were condemned for witchcraft. Although children and men were executed during Europe's witch hunt, the typical witch was female. The Devil preferred women.

It is impossible to say how many so-called witches were executed, but scholars know that at least two hundred thousand were burned at the stake.

Over two hundred thousand people accused of witchcraft were burned at the stake in Europe during the 16th and 17th centuries. This German woodcut made in 1555 depicts one such event.

The number of witch trials decreased during the eighteenth century. The last executions took place in Germany in 1775 and in Switzerland in 1782. Many brave writers risked their lives to denounce witch trials, but could not stop the madness. Why people permitted the horrible witch hunts is a mystery that has never been clearly understood.

British Witches

ENGLISH WITCHES

The rage against witches, which swept through Europe like a plague, infected England during the reign of Queen Elizabeth I. Witches, who had been just a minor problem before, suddenly loomed as a major threat to the government. In 1563, after advisors warned their Protestant ruler that Catholic witches were plotting against her, Queen Elizabeth issued a witchcraft act. It ordered judges to seek out, try, and condemn witches. This law started England's mad witch craze. During Queen Elizabeth's time 535 witch trials took place and 82 so-called witches were hanged.

It is hard to understand how judges could believe that a talking cat named Sathan was a witch's aid. Elizabeth Francis, accused of using this talking cat to make a child sick, was sentenced to a year in jail. Mother Waterhouse, a mentally ill widow, was hanged because she said she asked this supercat to rub against a man and, in that way, killed him.

Children's testimony was always welcome. Three people were hanged after five girls, between the ages of nine and thirteen, accused them of causing the illness and death of Lady Cromwell. In another case, an eight-year-old boy sent his mother to the gallows, claiming she was a witch.

After Queen Elizabeth died in 1603, the witch hunt became even more vicious. King James VI of Scotland became King James I of England. The new ruler was so fascinated by witches that in 1597 he had written *Demonology*, a book that became England's antiwitch guide.

Because he thought the old witchcraft act too mild, King James issued a new law against witches. It condemned to death anyone guilty of contacting an evil spirit. Even a "good witch" who used magic words or made medicines at home deserved to hang. King James' witchcraft act, which took effect in 1604, was not repealed until 1736, one hundred and thirty-two years later!

England's witch hunt was at its worst in 1645. The master of the hunt, Matthew Hopkins, was the self-appointed "Witchfinder General." He was the country's champion witch exterminator.

Hopkins made witch finding his profession. Charging twenty shillings per town, plus expenses, he gave his word that he would uncover nests of witches. How valuable his services seemed! After all, Hopkins let it be known that he possessed the Devil's list of all the witches in England. Hopkins used methods that were described in King James' *Demonology*, such as the *water test*.

The Water Test

The water test was supposed to prove whether or not someone was a witch. Victims were stripped, their arms were crossed, and their thumbs were tied to their big toes. Then they were hurled into ponds and streams. Ropes were looped around their waists so that they could be pulled to shore after the test. Those who managed to float were witches. Only the innocent sank to the bottom, often drowning because they were pulled out too late. After all, it was necessary to wait a while—just to be "dead sure" a victim was not going to rise to the surface.

Imps and Witch Marks

Most English witches were said to own *imps*, also called *familiars*. An imp was a demon in animal form that advised and helped a witch perform evil deeds. It fed on witches' blood. A *witch mark* was a spot on a witch's body made by an imp-vampire.

From a book published in 1647 entitled
Matthew Hopkins, Discoverie of Witches.
Hopkins is shown watching two witches and their imps.

Finding witch marks was a Hopkins specialty. The telltale spots could be found easily, because if they were pricked no blood came out and no pain was felt. Hopkins hired several assistants to help him jab long sharp needles into suspects. To improve his hunting record—and his profits—he even had a fake needle made. It worked the way trick daggers do that are used on stage. The long needle disappeared into a handle when pressed against the skin. Then when a so-called witch did not bleed or cry out in pain, Hopkins declared he had found an imp's witch mark.

In addition to needle-pricking, he used another method to find imp owners. He forced accused witches to sit cross-legged and tied to a stool for days at a time. The victim wasn't given anything to eat and wasn't allowed to fall asleep. One of Hopkins' helpers remained in the room watching for imps. Any insect that appeared would do.

Household pets, imaginary animals, even flies, spiders, and bees were accepted by the courts as witches' imps. One old woman was forced to confess her guilt after four flies buzzed into the room. Another woman, kept awake for two days and two nights, confessed that two butterflies she kept in a jar were really imps.

Hopkins' career ended after people were horrified by his treatment of Parson Lowes, an elderly vicar. Lowes was kept awake night after night and made to run back and forth until he hardly knew what he was saying or doing. The parson confessed that he had made a pact with the Devil and that imps named Tom, Flo, Bess, and Mary were his helpers. Although he later denied these statements, Lowes was hanged.

Hopkins was responsible for a mass hanging of nineteen women in one day in Chelmsford in 1645. Because of him at least sixty-eight so-called witches were hanged that year.

After 1646 witch-pricking and imp-watching were forbidden. Hopkins and other professional witch finders were out of business. The number of witch trials decreased to a trickle by 1700. The last person condemned to death in England was Jane Wenham, tried in 1712 but pardoned by the judge.

The English witch craze was mild compared with other countries. There were no horrible tortures like the rack or the thumbscrew, and convicted English witches were hanged, not burned at the stake. Although about a thousand people were hanged, and perhaps as many died at the hands of mad mobs, England's witch hunts did not produce the mass executions that took place in many European countries.

Ireland was spared the witch craze of the sixteenth and seventeenth centuries, but in Scotland torture chambers were built and many awful witch burnings took place.

SCOTTISH WITCHES

Scotland's Witchcraft Act of 1563 condemned not only witches but also anyone who consulted them. Confessions were not necessary; just hearsay that one was a witch was reason enough to start a trial.

Witch hunts really took hold when King James VI (later James I of England) took charge of the trial and torture of the North Berwick witches in 1590. About seventy persons were accused. Among them was John Fian, a schoolteacher, who was supposed to be the leader in a Devil's plot to drown the king. One woman declared that she saw Fian with two hundred other witches, sailing the ocean on sieves. By throwing a bound cat into the water

James VI, King of Scotland, was a
major figure in the persecution of
witches in Scotland and England.
Here he questions accused witches at their trial.

these sea-going sorcerers caused a storm that nearly wrecked King James' ship. Examiners found a Devil's mark under Fian's tongue. He was tortured, strangled, and burned. Many others were also hanged or burned.

Inspired by King James' *Demonology*, the town of Aberdeen condemned twenty-four men and women to burn in 1597. Their crimes included dancing with the Devil, souring milk, giving out love charms, causing family fights, and hurting people with the evil eye.

An insane woman named Isobel Gowdie summed up witch myths in her confessions. According to Isobel, she flew to a sabbat on a straw and then made a pact with the Devil. Her coven of thirteen witches used frogs the size of oxen to dig up and destroy a farmer's field. Isobel boasted that she was able to turn into a bird and that her friends appeared as cats and rabbits. She talked about imps named "Pickle-nearest-the-Wind," "Batter-them-down-Maggy," and "Able and Stout."

The last execution for witchcraft in Scotland took place in 1727, when Janet Horne was burned after being charged with changing her daughter into a flying horse. The poor woman was so crazed that she clapped her hands and laughed at the sight of the "bonnie fire," before she was thrown into its flames.

Witchcraft laws were repealed in both Scotland and England in 1736.

Witches in America

Settlers took the fear of witches with them from Europe to the American colonies. Almost everybody believed that a person could become a witch by making a pact with the Devil.

Outside of New England only one person was executed as a witch. She was Rebecca Fowler, hanged in Maryland in 1685. The colonists were more concerned about the dangerous "red devil" Indians than they were about imagined witches. A few witch trials did take place, but the accused were usually pardoned or spent only a short time in prison.

No witch trials were held in New York or Rhode Island. At New Hampshire's only witch case, the prisoner was set free after she promised to behave herself.

William Penn helped to keep a witch scare from spreading through Pennsylvania. Like most Quakers, he took a dim view of witchcraft. As acting judge, he told a confused old woman who confessed she could fly that she had a perfect right to ride her broomstick. There was no law against it. Penn dismissed the case.

The Devil made his home in New England. He lived in the minds of the Puritans who had settled in Connecticut and Massachusetts. Ministers constantly gave long sermons about the Devil and the tortures of Hell. Their warnings about sin and Satan were enough to frighten the wits out of anybody.

In 1642 Connecticut passed a law that stated that anyone who contacted a "familiar spirit" must be killed. Four witches were hanged in Connecticut. Massachusetts had a similar antiwitch law on its books after 1641.

The first victim was Margaret Jones, hanged in 1648 because she bewitched children and cured sick people, and because a witch mark was found on her body. About ten witch hangings and several witch trials had already taken place when the Devil discovered Salem in 1692. He made it his headquarters. All Hell broke loose.

SALEM, THE DEVIL'S HEADQUARTERS

The witch scare started in the home of Salem's minister, Reverend Samuel Parris. His nine-year-old daughter Betty and her eleven-year-old cousin Abigail were secretly learning forbidden "facts." Their teacher was Tituba, the family's West Indian slave. Tituba claimed to know about spells, chants, and fortune-telling. She was so wonderful to listen to that Betty and Abigail invited friends over to hear Tituba talk.

How exciting it was to look into a home-made crystal ball, made with the white of an egg suspended in a glass. The girls hoped that by peering into it they would see images of their future husbands. But their harmless fortune-telling ended with a horrible vision. The egg white in the glass took on "the likeness of a coffin." The girls were frightened sick!

Betty and Abigail began to show signs of a strange illness. They wept, barked like dogs, and screamed as though they were in terrible pain. They rolled on the floor as their bodies twitched and twisted. When these fits ended, they acted normally—until the next strange attack of madness. Prayers seemed to trigger fits. Abigail stamped her feet and covered her ears at prayer time. And Betty hurled a Bible across the room, sobbing that she was damned.

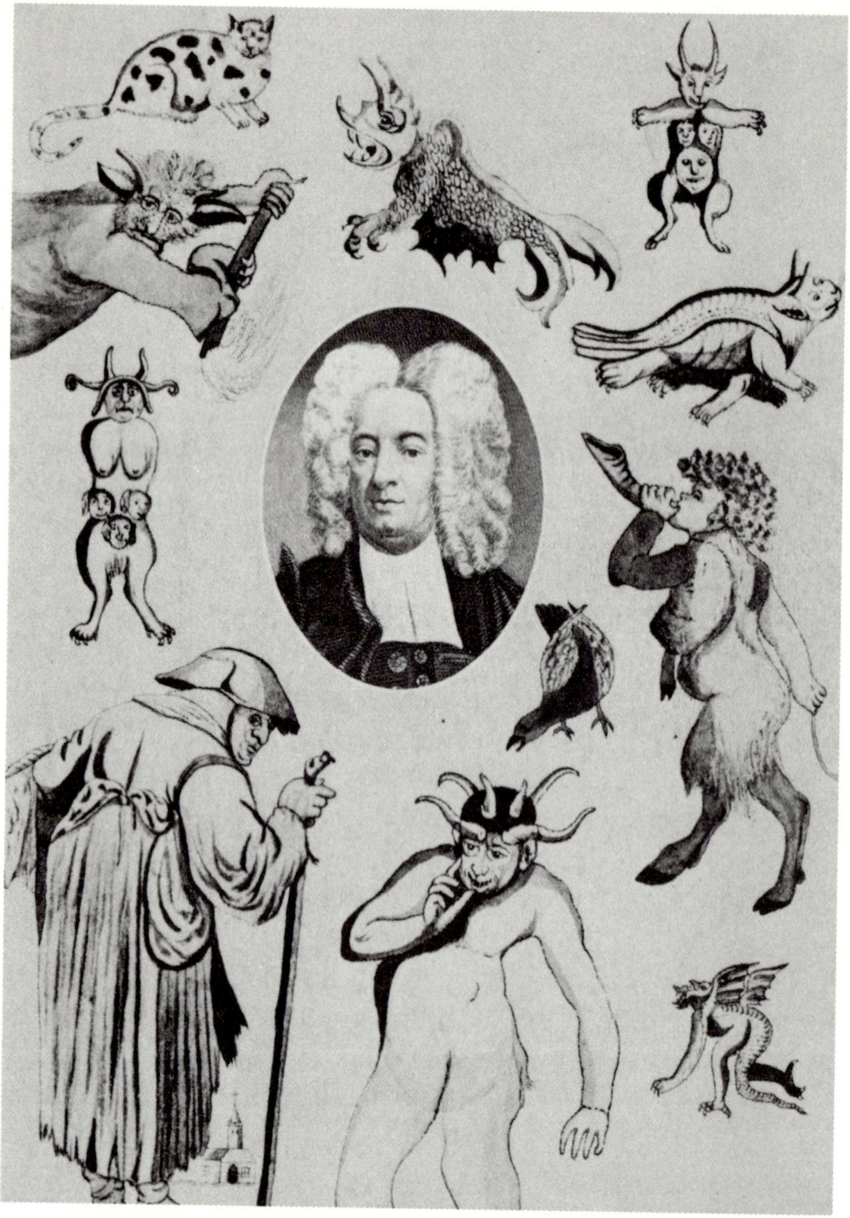

The alarmed Reverend Parris called in Dr. Griggs, the town physician. After hearing the girls scream and watching them roll and writhe on the floor, the doctor concluded that the problem was definitely not medical. "The evil hand is on them," he said. Church ministers were consulted. They decided that only the Devil, aided by witches, could have produced the strange sickness.

Within a month after Betty and Abigail started having fits, eight of their girl friends caught the puzzling disease. (Today we know that the girls were suffering from *contagious hysteria*. Groups of people can "infect" each other and copy each other's symptoms. This mental illness is often caused by extreme fear, guilt, and stress.)

The ministers decided that the girls must be urged to tell who was bewitching them. The girls did not want to accuse anyone, but the grown-ups of Salem insisted upon it. And so the girls started a roll call that grew and grew.

The Witch List
Tituba's name headed the list. Two others were accused: Sarah Good, a dirty, pipe-smoking beggar, and Sarah Osborne, a very

*Cotton Mather (1663–1728)
was a prominent minister who
wrote several books about
the Salem witchcraft trials.
He is shown here surrounded
by some forms thought to
be assumed by the devil.*

sick woman who hadn't been to church in months. The two Sarahs insisted they were innocent. Tituba, however, spent three days in court confessing her guilt. She was "urged" to do this after Reverend Parris whipped her. Tituba probably believed that by telling Salem what it wanted to hear, she was saving herself.

She described the Devil as "a thing all over hairy." She spoke about red cats and red rats that served her, and about a monster with a woman's face and wings. Tituba had even seen the Devil's book, which listed nine witches in Salem. How alarming! The courts only knew about three!

The three prisoners were sent to jail. Sarah Osborne died there. Sarah Good was hanged. As for Tituba, she remained locked up for thirteen months until she was sold as a slave by her jailers.

The girls' fits continued—sure proof that there were other witches in the land. They denounced one person after another. Men, women, and children were arrested. Four-year-old Dorcas Good, Sarah's little daughter, was thrown into a dungeon and chained to the walls, because the girls reported that she could change herself into a dog. Rebecca Nurse, seventy years old, sick and deaf, was accused of killing babies that had died years before. She was hanged. No one was safe. Even a clergyman ended up

The title page of The Wonders of the Invisible World, *by Cotton Mather, in which he wrote of the trials and executions of the Salem witches in 1692.*

The Wonders of the Invisible World:

Being an Account of the

TRYALS

OF

𝔖everal 𝔚itches,

Lately Excuted in

NEW-ENGLAND:

And of several remarkable Curiosities therein Occurring.

Together with,

I. Observations upon the Nature, the Number, and the Operations of the Devils.

II. A short Narrative of a late outrage committed by a knot of Witches in *Swede-Land*, very much resembling, and so far explaining, that under which *New-England* has laboured.

III. Some Councels directing a due Improvement of the Terrible things lately done by the unusual and amazing Range of *Evil-Spirits* in *New-England*.

IV. A brief Discourse upon those *Temptations* which are the more ordinary Devices of Satan.

By *COTTON MATHER.*

Published by the Special Command of his EXCELLENCY the Govenour of the Province of the *Massachusetts-Bay* in *New-England*.

Printed first, at *Bostun* in *New-England*; and Reprinted at London, for *John Dunton*, at the *Raven* in the *Poultry*. 1693.

A scene from a Salem witchcraft trial.

on the gallows. Reverend George Burroughs was named "the black minister" in charge of witches' sabbats, which took place in Reverend Parris' back yard. (Unlike the wild, party-like sabbats of Europe, Puritan witches sat quietly listening to long sermons from the Devil, and instead of eating babies, they dined on bread and cheese.)

Spooky Proof
The girls could accuse anyone they wished, because the Puritans believed in a spooky proof: that a witch's body could be at home while his or her image (spirit) could be roaming about hurting people.

The members of Parris' girls' club insisted they were being tortured by witches who never came in person but sent their spirits instead. No one challenged their statements, because the spirits were invisible. Only the bewitched and witches could see them. Thus, while old Rebecca Nurse lay ill in bed, her image roamed about pinching and kicking the girls. And Martha Cory, a respected churchgoer, was hanged because she used her image to torture the girls and bring on their fits.

The Touch Test
The touch test was a handy way of making sure that an accused witch was guilty. When the girls saw a so-called witch, they threw frightening fits. When a witch was made to touch them, these fits stopped. The touch test was so important that the girls were always kept within reach. They were given front-row seats at trials. Two of the group were sent on tour to Andover, Gloucester, and Boston with their "touch-and-tell" act. The girls were Massachusetts' official witch finders.

The wild witch hunt lasted from March to September 1692. It ended after the girls accused Lady Phips, the governor's wife, and Samuel Willard, the President of Harvard College. Then the judges concluded that the girls were not reliable after all! They had misled the courts and caused juries to make mistakes.

As a result of these "mistakes" nineteen were hanged, two died in prison, and one man was pressed to death with stones because he refused to talk. Over one hundred and forty-two had been arrested. Those who were in prison in September were set free—but only after they had paid for their room and board in prison.

In 1697 the entire jury, a judge, and one of the girls publicly confessed that they had condemned innocent people. They begged to be forgiven. In 1957 the Commonwealth of Massachusetts officially cleared the names of everyone who had been accused of witchcraft.

Witches Today

For hundreds of years now, no witches have been executed either in Europe or America. But the idea that there are witches in the world has never died. People who call themselves witches are more popular than ever. They don't have to hide from the public. Instead, they can boast about their witch tricks and tell the world about their powers through newspaper, radio, and TV interviews.

There are many different kinds of modern witches. The best known claim to be followers of an ancient religion called *Wicca*.

THE WITCH RELIGION

Wicca means *wise one* in Anglo-Saxon. Many people honestly believe that they can gain wisdom and witch power by signing up as members of Wicca, "The Old Religion."

The Wiccan movement was inspired by a book written by Margaret Murray in 1921. Murray claimed that many good witches were followers of a religion of nature worship that dates back to the Stone Age. This pagan religion was supposedly performed in secret during the centuries of witch hunts. According to her book, *The Witch Cult in Western Europe*, good witches have always held sabbats and formed covens in order to worship nature gods.

Margaret Murray's beliefs are not accepted by scholars today. There isn't any proof that witches were ever organized in the past. Yet, in the 1950s, a movement was set up to rediscover the pagan religion Murray described. It took off like a flying broomstick.

Gerald Gardner was its first leader. Calling himself the High Priest of Wicca, he wrote books and became a popular guest on radio and TV. Gardner inspired people in Europe and America to form witch clubs—modern covens.

Alex Sanders, known as the "king" of witches, is proof that witchcraft still enjoys a loyal following.

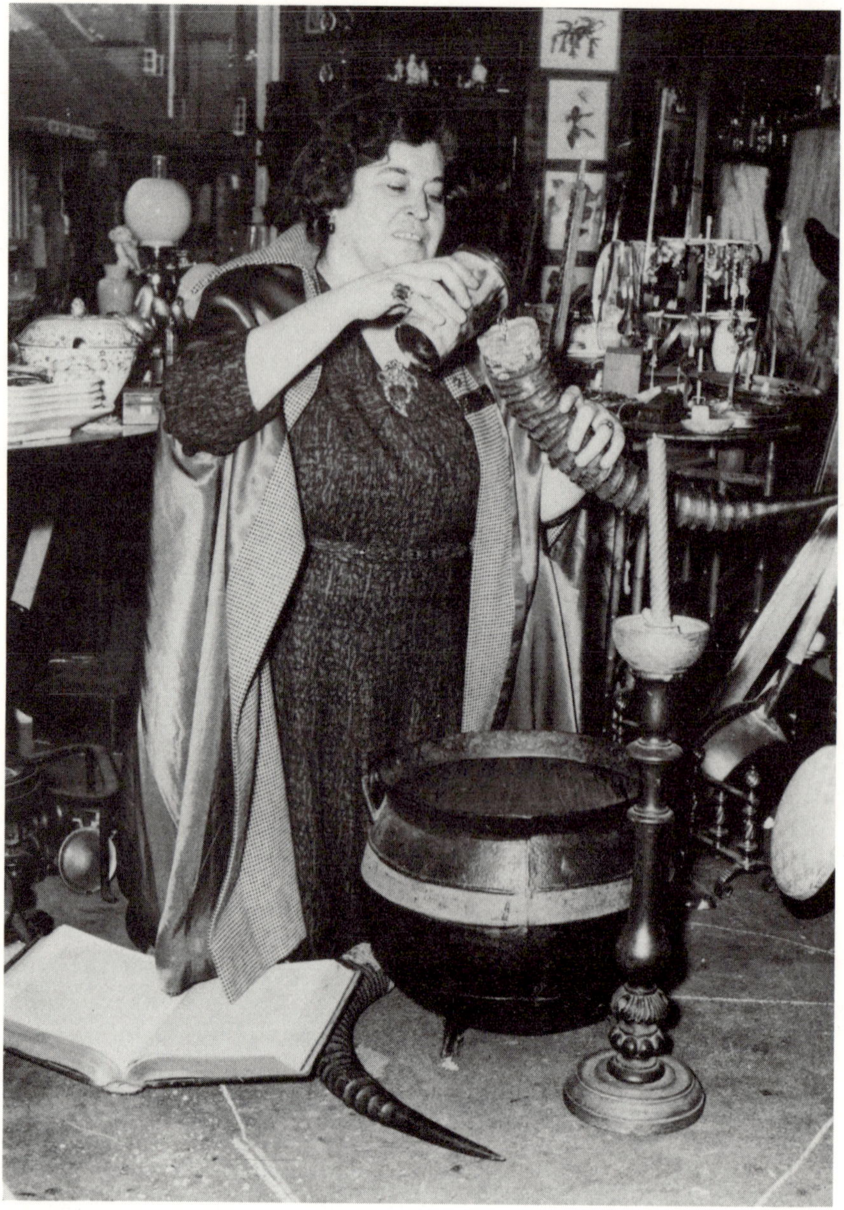

After Gardner's death in 1964, Alex Sanders became the most prominent High Priest. Sanders, also called the King of Witches, attracted a large following.

Sybil Leek, Wicca's wonder woman, became its best missionary. This former British antiques dealer made herself the most famous of all modern-day witches. Her frequent TV appearances and her many books described "what it takes to be a good witch and how to avoid bad ones." As a result, new witches kept popping up everywhere, especially in the United States and Britain.

Wicca followers don't serve the Devil. They can't shape-shift into animals or make broomsticks fly. They are "good" witches who, at their local witch clubs, or covens, worship a Moon Goddess and a Horned God.

The Modern Coven

Ceremonies vary from coven to coven. A high priest plus twelve other witches make up the usual modern coven. The troop gathers at midnight to perform secret ceremonies and murmur magical prayers. Their temple may be a basement, the back of a shop, or a member's living room. Most Wicca witches make sure the people next door know nothing about their night life. What "wise ones" they are!

Sybil Leek, who professes to be a "good witch," works on a "solution" in the antique shop she once owned in England.

The witches hold hands while standing around the rim of a 9-foot (2.74-m) circle drawn on the floor. They chant and pray. Candles flicker, wands wave, and bells ring to summon pagan gods. Cauldrons filled with liquid often bubble and boil in the middle of the magic circle. Some priests hold a *witch's wheel,* or *wheel of fortune,* whose spokes are decorated with signs of the zodiac. They turn the wheel like a sailor steering a ship as they sail their sea of sorcery. One New York coven rides broomsticks. Members solemnly hop around on them in the priest's basement, using the magic circle as their hobby-horse riding ring.

The Book of Shadows, the coven's top-secret book, is closely guarded by the high priest so that no outsiders ever see it. Each member signs the book and swears never to reveal its contents.

In many covens, new members are sworn in blindfolded with their wrists bound behind them with cords, which are also tied around their necks. A dagger is pointed over their hearts as they take their vows. The dagger is just a symbol of witchcraft; it's not a weapon meant to harm anyone. After being sworn in, new members are congratulated. They have become genuine witches.

Witches usually wear robes and special necklaces at their group sessions. But in some covens they prefer to worship *skyclad,* which means naked. They believe that clothes stop special energy rays from coming out of the body.

A coven is supposed to be able to raise a *cone of power,* which is the combined energy rays of the group, that can be strong enough to shape history. According to Wicca witch books, a coven's cone of power worked up a storm that helped Drake defeat the Spanish Armada, and another cone caused Napoleon's downfall. During World War II, witches supposedly met in Washington, D.C., to lay a curse on Hitler by sticking pins in a doll that looked like him. British witches did their share: they kept raising cones to make sure that Germans did not invade England.

When there isn't a national emergency witch covens raise cones to cure illnesses and stop any miseries reported by their members.

EVIL WITCHES

Not all covens are club-like, friendly gatherings. A few groups are bent on evil. They seem to enjoy frightening others and possibly frightening themselves. They hold Black Masses, which are Devil-worshipping services. Ministers of Satan lead prayers from *The Devil's Book*. In one California temple, skeletons are wall hangings, human skulls are candle holders, and tombstones are tables. The goings-on are top secret—except for those who pay a fee to join.

There are also wicked witches in private practice who sell curses and act out all sorts of mysterious rites for customers who want to hurt those they hate. They often use *image magic*: making a clay, wax, or wooden image of a victim and then sticking pins into it, destroying it with a knife, or burning it. This is supposed to cause pain, burns, and even death to the person represented by the image. Photographs of enemies are pricked, torn, and burned. Harmful magic is also tried with a piece of clothing, a lock of hair, or fingernail clippings of the hated person.

Gamblers have hired modern witches for the evil-eye power, which they use against boxers and baseball and football teams. When the *whammy*, or eye curse, doesn't work, there's no pay-off for anybody.

Witches held a First World Congress of Sorcery in Bogota,

Colombia, in 1975. Newspapers reported that thousands were disappointed because the Devil failed to attend.

TRIBAL WITCHES

Tribes living in the jungles of Africa, the deserts of America, and the mountains of Asia believe in witches. Strangely enough, their witch myths are like those that haunted Europe and New England long ago.

According to the Pueblo Indians of New Mexico and the Bantu tribesmen of Africa, witches fly about at night, holding lights that flicker like fireflies. They also shape-shift. American Indian witches turn themselves into cats, bears, and owls. African witches become baboons, lions, and leopards. And South American sorcerers turn themselves into jaguars.

Imps are also part of modern tribal witchlore. Watersnakes, bats, termites, and grasshoppers are among the many creatures that serve as witches' companions and helpers.

Although witch doctors perform magic, they are not usually looked upon as harmful witches. They try to use supernatural powers to cure anyone cursed by witches. And they hand out ointments and charms that are supposed to keep witches away.

Witch doctors also act as witch detectives. Some "smell out" a suspect by sniffing around a village. Others dance themselves into a trance and then point to the men and women who could be witches.

Suspected witches are sometimes asked to move away or to apologize for hurting someone. A witch doctor may hand out medicines that accused witches must drink. The medicine is meant to prevent them from continuing to perform witchcraft.

This oil painting done in 1832 by George Catlin shows an American Indian medicine man in a "curing" costume.

Tribal witches are not accused of worshipping the Devil. In many areas, people feel sorry for them because they can't help their witch "condition." They were just born that way. One African tribe believes that all witches have a growth in their stomachs called a *mangu*. Another tribe is sure that witches have pythons in their stomachs. Only witch-doctor medicine can control the *mangu* and kill the python.

What strange beliefs! But are they any stranger than those held by people in the so-called civilized part of the world?

THE WITCH BUSINESS

Witch business is big business. European and American witches are cashing in. They don't deal with devils and demons. They deal with you. Today's witches promise to bring happiness and good luck to cash customers.

Books by modern witches are selling faster than you can say "bat's blood." A book advertisement states, "Whatever it is you need or want, witchcraft can get it for you quickly and easily." Witch books explain how to find friends, attract lovers, and make people do whatever you want them to do. The American reader can even learn how to cut down on doctors' bills. There are books that reveal how to "heal yourself as witches do."

Reading isn't the only way to learn witch secrets. All sorts of do-it-yourself witch kits are on sale. Stores in London, New York, and other big cities sell graveyard dust, bats' hearts, jellied cats' eyes, swallows' skeletons, and black-cat bones—with instruction sheets.

A witch's candle shop sells *Death Unto Mine Enemy* (Dume) candles. Just burn one, and the powers of the person you hate will melt away. Light white candles for good health; green ones for money; red candles for finding lovers; and black ones for cursing others.

Mail-order witch businesses have customers all over the world. John-the-Conquerer Oil, sure to make the girls swoon, is a big seller. A Magic Money Jar with a magic magnet that attracts money actually works—but only for the mail-order house. A Black Mirror should be the best buy of all. By looking into it, the owner sees the future. The catalogue states that "one man uses it to read tomorrow's newspaper."

There are also voodoo doll kits (pins included). All you have to do is stick pins into the doll while you think about someone you hate. Your enemy will have "pins and needles" until you stop.

For those who aren't satisfied with assorted witch tricks, there are correspondence courses that will make them full-time witches. One American witch school offers a doctorate degree in witchcraft. Just sign up for their eighty-dollar mail-order lessons. Witches who want to earn graduate degrees can take advanced study—after advancing more cash. They receive diplomas that make them high priests or witch bishops.

Some people want to become witches because they seek thrills and excitement. Others hope that by joining a coven they will learn how to use supernatural powers. Many lonely, unhappy, unsuccessful people feel important when they join a secret society.

People want magic in their lives. How wonderful to own items that bring health, wealth, and happiness. Who needs a fairy godmother or a magic lantern, when modern witchcraft promises to make wishes come true? Self-styled witches, through books, shops, and mail-order companies, offer dreams for sale. They are cashing in on the oldest superstitions in the world.

Glossary

Chant A song that is supposed to have magical powers—also called *incantation*.

Charm An object worn for its supposed magical powers.

Cone of Power A cone, or peak, of power formed by witches' body rays, that is supposedly able to change events.

Coven A group of witches usually having a leader and twelve members.

Demon An evil spirit ruled by the Devil.

Devil Ruler of evil. Also called *Satan*.

Devil's Mark A mark made on the witch's body by the Devil.

Evil Eye An eye or glance that is supposed to bring bad luck.

Familiar A demon in animal form that, supposedly, helps witches: an *imp*.

Heretic A person who does not agree with accepted beliefs. During the witch hunts a heretic was one who did not believe in all the Christian teachings.

Hysteria A mental illness caused by extreme fear, guilt, and stress. People can infect each other and copy each other's actions. Group hysteria is called *contagious hysteria*.

Image Magic Hurting an enemy by hurting a doll, statue, picture, or any image of that enemy.

Imp A demon in animal form that supposedly advises and helps a witch perform evil deeds. Also called a *familiar*.

Inquisition An investigation that was set up by the Roman Catholic church. Its aim was to find and punish people who didn't believe in all the teachings of the church.

Pact with the Devil A contract signed in witch's blood between the Devil and the witch. The witch agreed to worship and serve the Devil. The Devil agreed to give the witch supernatural powers to perform evil.

Shape-shifting Changing from human shape into the shape of an animal or another person.

Sabbat A large meeting of witches to worship the Devil.

Satan Another word for Devil.

Sorcerer A magician or a witch.

Spell A spoken word or group of words believed to have magical powers.

Warlock A male witch, also known as *wizard*.

Whammy Slang word, meaning *curse*.

Wicca "The Old Religion," adopted by modern witches, who claim it dates back to the Stone Age, when people had nature gods.

Witch A person supposedly able to harm or help others through magical, supernatural powers.

Witch's Mark A spot, or mark, on a witch's body made by an imp sucking witch's blood.

Witch's Wheel A wheel whose spokes are decorated with signs of the zodiac. It is used by Wicca priests for fortune-telling. Also called *wheel of fortune*.

Wizard A warlock; a male witch.

Bibliography

Alderman, Clifford L. *Witchcraft in America*. New York: Julian Messner, 1974.
Baroja, Julio Caro. *The World of Witches*. Chicago: University of Chicago Press, 1975. (Available in United Kingdom.)
Booth, Sally Smith. *The Witches of Early America*. Hastings-on-Hudson, New York: Hastings House, 1975.
Boyer, Paul, and Nissenbaum, Stephen. *Salem Possessed*. Cambridge, Mass.: Harvard University Press, 1974. (Available in United Kingdom.)
Cohn, Norman. *Europe's Inner Demons*. New York: The New American Library, 1975. London: Heinemann Educational Books, 1976.
Freedland, Nat. *The Occult Explosion*. New York: Berkley Publishing Corporation, 1972.
Haining, Peter. *Witchcraft and Black Magic*. New York: Bantam Books, 1973. Middlesex, England: Hamlyn Publishing Group, Ltd., 1971.
Hansen, Chadwick. *Witchcraft at Salem*. New York: George Braziller, Inc., 1969. London: Arrow Books, 1971.

Hole, Christina. *Witchcraft in England.* New York: Charles Scribner's Sons, 1947. London: Batsford, Ltd., 1977.

Holmes, Ronald. *Witchcraft in History.* Secaucus, N.J.: Citadel Press, 1974. London: Miller (Frederick) Ltd., 1974.

Hughes, Pennethorne. *Witchcraft.* Middlesex, England: Penguin Books, Ltd., 1965.

Kramer, Henry, and Sprenger, Jackob. *The Hammer of Witches.* London: Folio Society, 1968.

Leek, Sybil. *The Complete Art of Witchcraft.* New York: The New American Library, 1971. London: Freewin Books Ltd., 1975.

Mackay, Charles. *Extraordinary and Popular Delusions and the Madness of Crowds.* London: Richard Bentley, 1841. New York: The Noonday Press, 1932. London: Allen & Unwin, 1973.

Mair, Lucy. *Witchcraft.* New York: World University Library, 1969. London: Weidenfeld & Nicolson, 1969.

Maple, Eric. *The Complete Book of Witchcraft and Demonology.* Cranbury, N.J.: A.S. Barnes & Co., 1962.

Marwick, Max. *Witchcraft and Sorcery.* Middlesex, England: Penguin Books, Ltd., 1970.

Newell, Venetia. *The Encyclopaedia of Witchcraft and Magic.* New York: A & W Visual Library, 1974.

Robbins, Rossell H. *The Encyclopaedia of Witchcraft and Demonology.* New York: Crown Publishers, Inc., 1959.

Starkey, Marion L. *The Devil in Massachusetts.* New York: Alfred Knopf, Inc., 1949.

Trevor-Roper, Hugh. *The European Witch-Craze.* New York: Harper Torchbooks, 1969.

JUVENILE BOOKS

Garden, Nancy. *Witches*. Philadelphia, Pa.: J.B. Lippincott, 1975.
Hoyt, Olga. *Witches*. New York: Abelard-Schuman, 1972.
Kohn, Bernice. *Out of the Cauldron*. New York: Holt, Rinehart & Winston, 1972.
O'Connell, Margaret. *The Magic Cauldron*. New York: S.G. Phillips, 1975.

Index

Accusers, of witches, 15, 19, 21, 35–42
Africa, 50, 52
American witches, 33–42, 47
Ancient witches, 5–10
Animals, witches as, 27–30, 32, 47, 50

Babylonia, 5
Black Masses, 49
Book of Shadows, The, 48
British witches, 26–30, 47
Broomsticks, 48
Burnings, witch, 9, 12, 18, 19, 21, 32. *See also* Executions, Hangings
Burroughs, Rev. George, 41
Business, witch, 52–53

Carpzov, Judge Benedict, 12
Ceremonies, modern, 47, 48
Chants, 6, 48
Children, as witnesses, 18, 26, 35–42
Cone of power, 48, 49
Confessions, 19, 21, 30, 32, 38
Connecticut, 34

Contagious hysteria, 37
Cory, Martha, 41
Court decisions, on witches, 12, 15, 19, 21, 42
Covens, 18, 32, 53
    evil, 49–50
    modern, 44, 47–49
Curses, 2, 6, 49

Death
    sentences, 9, 12, 18, 21–22, 26, 27, 32, 38
    toll, 22–24
Death Unto Mine Enemy (Dume) candles, 52–53
Demonology (King James I), 26, 27
Demonology (Remy), 12, 32
Devil
    descriptions of, 38
    mark, 19, 32
    Pact with, 15–16, 19, 29, 32, 34
    supernatural powers received from, 9, 10, 15, 47
Devil's Book, The, 49

Egypt, 5
Elizabeth I, Queen of England, 26
Evil eye, 2, 32, 49
Evil witches, 49–50
Examining witches, 19–21
Executions, 9, 10, 12, 18, 19, 21–22, 24, 26, 29, 30, 32, 34, 35, 38. *See also* Burnings, Hangings

Fasting, 9
Fian, John, 30–32
First World Congress of Sorcery, 49–50
Flade, Judge Dietrich, 15
Folk witches, 9
Fowler, Rebecca, 34
France, 12, 22
Future, forecasting of, 6

Gardner, Gerald, 44, 47
Germany, 19, 21, 22, 24
Good, Sarah, 37, 38
Gowdie, Isobel, 32
Greece, 6

Halloween, 2
Hammer of Witches, The, (Kramer and Sprenger), 12, 21
Hangings, witch, 10, 26, 29, 32, 34, 35, 38. *See also* Burnings, Executions
Hebrews, 6
Hecate, 6
Heretics, 9
High Priest of Wicca, 44, 47, 48

Hopkins, Matthew, 27, 29, 30

Image magic, 49
Imps, 27–30, 32, 50
Indians, American, 34
Inquisition, effect on witch hunts, 9
Insanity, 15

James I, King of England, 26, 27, 30
  as King James VI of Scotland, 30, 32
Jones, Margaret, 34–35

Kramer, Henry, 12

Lawyers, 15
Leek, Sybil, 47
Love potions, 2, 6

Mail-order witch businesses, 53
Mass executions, 10
Massachusetts, 34, 35, 38, 41
Media, 44, 47
Missionaries, 9
Murray, Margaret, 44

New England, witches in, 34–37
Nurse, Rebecca, 38, 41

Osborne, Sarah, 37, 38

Pact with the Devil, 15–16, 19, 29, 32, 34
Pagan gods, supernatural powers received from, 9

Parris girls, as official witch finders, 35–42
Parris, Rev. Samuel, 35, 37, 38, 41
Penn, William, 34
Phips, Lady, 42
Plague, 10
Poisons, 2, 6
Puritans, 34, 41

Religion, witch, 44–47
Remy, Judge Nicholas, 12
Rome, 9

Sabbat, 16–18, 19, 32, 41, 44
Salem witch hunt, 35–42
Sanders, Alex, 47
Scottish witches, 30–32
Sentencing witches, 9, 12, 18, 21–22
Shape-shifting, 5, 47, 50
Skyclad worship, 48
Spells, 2, 16
Spooky proof, 41
Sprenger, Jackob, 12
Sweden, 18
Switzerland, 22, 24

Television, 44, 47
Tituba, 35, 37, 38
Torture, 9, 12, 19, 21, 30, 32
Touch test, 41
Trials, 12, 15, 19, 21, 24, 30, 32, 34, 35
Tribal witches, 50–52

UFOs, 16

Vampires, 27, 29

Voodoo, 48, 49, 53

Warlocks, 5
Water test, 27
Whammy, 49
Wheel of fortune, 48
Wiccan movement, 44–48
Willard, Samuel, 42
Windbags, 6
Witch Cult in Western Europe, The, (Murray), 44
Witch doctors, 50, 52
Witch hunts
  effect of Inquisition on, 9
  Salem, 35–42
Witch marks, 27–30, 35
Witch-pricking, 27–30
Witch religion, 44–47
Witchcraft Act of 1563 (Scotland), 30
Witchcraft
  degrees in, 53
  laws, repeal of, 32
Witches
  American, 33–42, 47
  ancient, 5–10
  British, 26–30, 47
  definition of, 2, 5, 9
  good and bad, 2, 5, 6, 27, 47, 49–50
  modern, 43–53
  Scottish, 30–32
Witch's wheel, 48
Wizards, 5
Women, as witches, 5, 22

Zodiac signs; 48